'A bettre envyned man was no-wher noon.
With-oute bake mete was never his hous,
Of fish and flesh, and that so plenteous,
It snewed in his hous of mete and drinke,
Of alle deyntees that men coude thinke,
After the sondry sesons of the yeer,
So chaunged he his mete and his soper.
Ful many a fat partich hadde he in mewe,
And many a breem and many a luce in stewe,
Wo was his cook, but-if his sauce were
Poynaunt and sharp, and redy al his gere.'

Geoffrey Chaucer, *c.* 1340–1400, *Prologue*; *Canterbury Tales*,
description of the Franklin

MEDIEVAL COOKERY

Recipes & History

by
Maggie Black

with a Foreword by
Loyd Grossman OBE

ENGLISH HERITAGE

Front cover: John of Gaunt, Duke of Lancaster, dining with the King of Portugal, depicted in a late 15th-century manuscript

Endpapers: Cooking and serving food in the 14th century

Published by English Heritage, Kemble Drive, Swindon SN2 2GZ

Copyright © English Heritage and Maggie Black
First published 1985
Revised edition 2003

ISBN 1 85074 867 5

C60, 1/04, Product code 50817

Edited by Susan Kelleher
Designed by Pauline Hull
Picture research by Elaine Willis
Brought to press by Andrew McLaren and Elaine Pooke
Printed in England by Bath Press

CONTENTS

FOREWORD

Would the pyramids have been built without the recently invented bread to efficiently feed the workforce? Food is a common denominator between us all, and a potent link with our ancestors, just as much as an ancient parish church or a listed house.

I am delighted to contribute a Foreword to English Heritage's series of historic cookery books, which neatly combine two of my passions – history and food. Most of us no longer have to catch or grow our own food before eating it, but the continuing daily need for sustenance still powerfully links us with our earliest forebears. We may not like the thought of Roman fish sauce made with fermented entrails (until we next add oyster sauce to a Chinese beef dish), but we can only sigh with recognition at a Jacobean wife's exhortation to 'let yor butter bee scalding hott in yor pan' before pouring in the beaten eggs for an omelette. The Roman penchant for dormice cooked in milk doesn't resonate with us now, but a dish of pears in red wine features at modern dinner parties just as it did in medieval times.

Food and cooking have inevitably changed down the centuries, as modern cookers have supplanted open hearths, and increased wealth and speedy transport have opened up modern tastes and palates to the widest range of ingredients and cuisines. But it's worth remembering that it was the Romans who gave us onions, sugar was an expensive luxury in the 16th century as was tea in the 17th, the tomato only became popular in Europe in the 19th century and even in the 1950s avocados and red peppers were still exotic foreign imports.

I urge you to experiment with the recipes in these books which cover over 2,000 years, and hope you enjoy, as I have, all that is sometimes strange and often familiar about the taste of times past.

Loyd Grossman OBE
Former Commissioner of English Heritage
Chairman of the Campaign for Museums

INTRODUCTION

The earliest surviving English recipe books date from about 1390 when *The Forme of Cury* was written by order of King Richard II. Our knowledge of English medieval cooking in general comes mostly from indirect sources, such as government and church regulations, account and rent books, and a few books about table manners and diet. Pictures and poems such as Chaucer's *Canterbury Tales* fill further social detail.

The recipes included in this book date from the late 14th and early 15th century and have been adapted for the modern kitchen. The following description about the type of food available at the time is useful to read first, and later in the book are articles revealing the cooking methods used in medieval England and the importance of table manners and etiquette.

Opposite: Nuts were an ingredient in a number of recipes in the late 14th and early 15th century

FOOD CHOICE

Bread was everyone's staple food in medieval England but the grain it was made from varied from place to place and according to one's income. Wheat made the finest, whitest bread but, as it only grew on good soil, only the lord of the manor, the feudal holder of a large estate, could afford to have land dug over and manured for it. The commonest bread, called maslin, was made from wheat and rye flour mixed together, while darker loaves were made from rye flour alone. Barley and other oats were the breadcorns of the north and west where the climate was wet and cold. Weed seeds were nearly always included in any grain and, when the harvest was poor, beans, peas and even acorns were used in the cheapest bread.

The main types of bread were:

White Breads

Pandemain or **paynemaine** – the finest quality bread made from flour sifted two or three times.

Wastel – another first-quality bread made from well-sifted flour.

Cocket – a slightly cheaper white bread which was replaced around 1500 with small loaves or rolls of top quality white bread called manchets (hand-sized breads).

Other Breads

Cheat or **whole wheat bread** – whole wheat bread with the coarse bran removed.

Tourte (or **trete** or **treet**) – contained husk as well as flour and may have been the bread used for trenchers (see below). Also known as brown bread.

Maslin, mesclin or **miscellin** – mixed wheat and rye bread.

Horse bread – peas, beans, and any other grain to hand were used.

There were also the cheap breads 'of all grains' which included bran bread (made mostly with bran) and, in the north and west especially, various kinds of barley bread and oatcakes which are still called havercakes or clapbread.

The most important use of brown bread for the wealthy was as trenchers (plates). The trenchers were made by cutting large loaves, preferably four days old, into thick slices with a slight hollow in the centre. An ordinary person would have only one or two plate trenchers for a whole meal, but a great personage would have several stacked up for him. These trenchers were gathered up in a basket and given to the poor after dinner.

Plain or toasted bread was used a great deal in cooked dishes. Breadcrumbs were a standard way of thickening sauces and of stiffening custards so that they could be sliced. Gingerbread was just a heavily spiced breadcrumb and honey mixture, often decorated with box leaves stuck on with whole cloves. Other cakes and buns were really just sweetened, spiced pieces of bread dough.

Most country people baked their own bread, but in the towns, professional bakers operated and were notorious as crafty swindlers. Therefore, in 1267, a set of regulations for assessing bread prices was laid down by royal order. Called the Assize of Bread, it tried to make sure that everyone paid a fair price for a loaf and no more. It was

Bread cakes – a basic food in the early medieval period

difficult to enforce, especially in small rural markets, but bakers who were caught flouting it were punished severely, and it was at least a responsible attempt to see that ordinary people could afford a very basic product.

Poorer people had another grievance besides bread prices. By about 1350, servants and serfs were complaining that they were only issued with coarse maslin or brown bread, and free labourers also resented not getting wheaten bread. Their masters justified it by saying that branny brown bread sustained those who did heavy manual work for long hours, but that it caused wind in people who lived sedentary lives. In fact, they really reserved it because it was a status symbol.

Fish was almost as vital as bread to medieval people. The Roman Catholic Church, to which everyone belonged, laid down that on Fridays (and until late in the period, Saturdays and Wednesdays) no one might eat meat. During Lent they were also forbidden to eat eggs and other dairy foods. This meant that for about half the days in the year everyone had to eat fish.

Opposite: Brown bread could be used for trenchers as well as eaten

Churchmen had even more restricted meals. Officially, the Rule of St Benedict forbade 'the meat of quadrupeds' to monks except for the sick, but from the 13th century the dietary strictures were respected less and less, and by the 15th century were usually honoured only at formal banquets.

For ordinary people, fish meant salted or pickled herrings. England's herring fleet caught thousands of fish throughout the summer, and there was a big salting and pickling industry to process them as this was the only way to preserve them for travel inland. Apart from dried cod, called stockfish, which was as hard as board, poor people inland got no other sea fish. Londoners

A 12th-century fish-day meal. The man in the centre is ready with a knife and trencher, while the page holds a beaker which will be shared by the guests

and people living near the east coast were luckier because they could get oysters and whelks quite cheaply.

In summer, when Lent was past, ordinary people inland could also vary their diet by catching river fish and collecting eels. The wealthy had a wider choice of sea fish, including those we know now, such as plaice, haddock and mackerel, as well as more exotic ones. Seals were eaten, and so were the 'royal' fish (whale, sturgeon and porpoise) which belonged to the king but which he often gave away. Shellfish such as crab and lobster were common and popular.

Landowners enjoyed plentiful supplies of river fish such as salmon, trout, grayling, bream and tench. Most estates of any size also had their own fishponds, called stews, in which they bred carp (a luxury) and pike (fairly common). Pickled salmon was a luxury imported from Scotland and Ireland when out of season at home.

One would think that this gave enough choice, even for the large number of 'fish days' in the year – but there were other, rather curious animals which were also classified as 'fish'. For instance, barnacle geese and puffins were alleged to be 'fish' because they were said to be created at sea, while beavers, which still existed in Britain, were said to have fishes' tails!

Since so much salt fish had to be eaten, many spice and herb sauces were developed specially to serve with them. Fried parsley was already a favourite garnish for fish.

Throughout medieval times more sheep were kept in eastern England than cattle. The Normans gave sheep-meat the name we know it by now – mutton (from '*mouton*', the French word for sheep). It was second favourite to beef, but both these red meats were preferred to the white meats of veal and kid as they made more solid, satisfying roasts. Goats were also kept for milk and meat.

A pig was a poor man's standby because the pig could forage for himself year-round in the woods, and fight off most foes. It looked and behaved like a wild pig, but when slaughtered the flesh made good pickling pork or bacon, the poor man's only winter meat. The 'innards' made blood puddings and other sausages, and the fat could be eaten on bread or used for cooking.

Cattle, sheep and goats, unlike swine, could not feed themselves throughout the winter, so fodder was a constant problem. As a result, all beasts (except breeding stock and milk animals) were slaughtered at intervals throughout the winter to provide fresh offal and salted joints. Beef sides, or goat and mutton

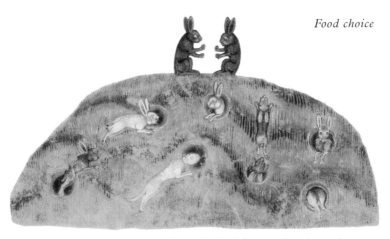

An illustration from the 14th-century Luttrell Psalter showing a 'pillow mound' – such mounds were built by warreners as artificial homes for rabbits in order to supply a ready source of meat

hams, were salted and smoked like pork. Fresh mutton could be roasted if young, but was better boiled if elderly. A medieval sheep was about the same size as our well-aged lamb. All domesticated animals were small, scrubby creatures, very different and much less meaty than today's specially-bred animals.

Game animals were designated personal property by the first Norman kings and nobles, and poachers were mutilated or executed if caught. But although hunting the wild bull, boar and deer remained an aristocratic privilege, hares and adult rabbits, which were called coneys, were made poor men's prey and free meat at the beginning of the 13th century. Wild cattle were getting rare, but boars were common almost until Tudor times and provided traditional Christmas brawn for all large feudal households. Roasting cuts of venison and pasties were 'top table' fare, but 'umbles' (liver and lights) made pies for the huntsmen and the lower tables at a household feast.

Poultry, game birds, small birds and waterfowl were enjoyed by everyone, especially the clergy, who were officially allowed to eat 'two-legged' but not 'four-legged' meat.

Apart from hunting wildfowl with falcons, a noble household would employ its own bird-catcher or bargain with a local poulterer for supplies, and would also have its own dovecote and domestic poultry yard (for pheasants and partridges as well as hens, ducks and geese). Some of this backyard stock might be cooped and fattened – battery rearing and force-feeding were common. Even the poor kept chickens, but eggs were precious, and so they would catch a wild bird or two to eat rather than kill their own hens.

Opposite: Eggs were an important part of the medieval diet and were known as 'white meat'

The birds which were eaten in medieval times were much more varied than we eat today. Swan or peacock were served at a banquet or celebration, dressed up as a processional centrepiece for the top table. The bustard was another 'great fowle' for parties. These enormous birds could weigh up to 12 kilos (25lbs) and could hardly fly. Other unusual meat choices were: crane, heron (especially the young ones called heronshewes), gull, curlew, egret, quail, plover, snipe, blackbird (the most expensive of the 'smale byrdes'), lapwing, thrush, bittern and greenfinch. Dishes of birds like these were served at almost all well-to-do meals, lay or clerical. At a feast, there might be as many as twenty dishes.

The milk of cows, sheep and goats alike was used throughout medieval times, although cow's milk came to be used most towards 1500 because it was less work to milk one cow than ten sheep. The milk and the cream, butter and cheese made from it, together with eggs, were called 'white meats'.

On large feudal estates, the milk was turned into cream, curds, soft cheese and butter for the lord's kitchen, and the residual whey and buttermilk made hard, skim-milk cheese for the servants and workers. This skim-milk cheese was sometimes so hard that it had

Sing a song of sixpence, a pocket full of rye,

Four and twenty blackbirds baked in a pie,

When the pie was opened, the birds began to sing,

Oh, wasn't that a dainty dish to set before the king?

There have been all sorts of interesting but improbable ideas about the origins of this ancient rhyme. One theory claims that it is a pirate recruiting song and refers to the infamous pirate named Blackbeard who used to pay his recruits sixpence a day and a pocketful (bottle) of rye (whisky)! Other suggestions are that it refers to the Cato Street Conspiracy of 1820 when a group of men plotted to murder the entire Cabinet at dinner one night. When they were discovered many of them began to tell about the others in the hope of saving themselves (the birds began to sing). However, the lines were known well before this date and may be a reference to a sumptuous banquet given in 1454 to members of the Order of the Golden Fleece, an order of knighthood founded by the Duke of Burgundy. An enormous pie was presented at the feast and when it was cut, 24 musicians emerged to play for the guests.

to be soaked and then beaten with a hammer before it could be eaten!

Well-to-do adults thought fresh milk was a drink only fit for children, the old and invalids, although they enjoyed thick rich cream and curdled cream – alone or with strawberries (against their doctors' advice!). They also thought butter was unwholesome

Sheep were a valuable source of food as they provided both meat and milk

for grown men to eat from midday onward, although children got bread and butter for breakfast and supper.

However, cooked dairy foods were another matter. Milk made hot beverages called possets or caudles, as well as cream soups and delicious custards. Cream made even richer ones. Soft, rich cream cheese called ruayn or rewain cheese made cheesecakes much like ours to supplement the rich man's meat dishes.

Even a medieval peasant kept a cow if he could, and unlike his lord he relied on it for food. Curds and whey, buttermilk, heavily salted butter and cheese were his staples. In summer he made soft cheese called spermyse or 'green' cheese. Bread and hard skim-milk cheese (which kept all winter) were his daily diet in the fields, as he ploughed, sowed and harvested the vital breadcorn.

In medieval times, everyone, high or low, ate pottage daily. This was broth or stock in which meat and/or vegetables had been boiled, with chopped meat, herbs and very often cereals or pulses added. The result was a soup-stew rather like Scotch broth.

The pottage might be thick (running) or almost thick enough to slice (stondyng). One well-known thick cereal pottage was frumenty and other thick, more luxurious pottages were called

mortrews. A peasant made do with pease pottage which was rather like runny pease pudding.

The commonest pottages, however, were vegetable ones, made with red or green cabbage, lettuces, leeks, onions and garlic, as in the recipe for lange wortys de chare (see page 39). Leek pottage, or white porray as it was called, was especially popular, and was thickened with ground almonds for the rich in Lent. Green porray, made with green vegetables and flavoured with parsley and other herbs, was also eaten a great deal. A green herb pottage simmering over the fire must have smelt delicious. Sadly, it was probably over-boiled and not very nourishing. Various kinds of roots from the garden might be added to pottage, such as turnips, carrots and rape (now only a field crop for oil), but potatoes were not known.

Any medieval garden contained a wide variety of 'potherbs' (vegetables 'for the pot') and flavouring herbs because they were used so much for medicine as well as cooking. Salad vegetables also had an important place in the garden and the recipe on page 47 uses only a few of the ones generally grown.

Opposite: Boiling bones as a base for pottage

One attractive idea, which has recently become popular again, was the use of flowers in salads. Primroses, violets and borage flowers were often added, and fruit and roots were often pickled and added to salads as well. Apples and pears, including the large hard pears called wardens, were usually cooked rather than eaten raw. 'Roasted' (baked) apples were very popular.

Citrus fruits began to be imported around 1290, and soon lemons were used both fresh and pickled, as well as Seville oranges. Both were very expensive. However, sweet lemon preserves were bought from importers and, later, English housewives learnt to make their own.

Other imports, reserved at first almost entirely for the rich because of their price, were currants, raisins, figs, dates and prunes. Dried fruit together with spices created the character of

The vibrant hues of borage and violet flowers made an attractive decoration for salads

typical medieval feast food. Dishes for the wealthy were full of them, and poorer people generally got some at Christmas and for feast-days.

The biggest luxury import was almonds. On fast-days, ground almonds could be substituted for pounded chicken as a thickening, or diluted to make a substitute for cow's milk. Almond milk features in dozens of recipes. The poor had to make do with oatmeal, but in season, they could gather and use or store wild hazelnuts and cobs as a useful addition to their diet.

We owe cane sugar to the Crusaders who tasted it in the East just before 1100. It was imported ready processed in the form of cones called loaves – white if refined and fairly pure, or dirty brown. However, it was so rare and expensive even at the end of the medieval period that it was treated as a spice and kept under lock and key if possible.

Salt had been mined in England since early times, and was also made from evaporated sea water. Apart from the tons used for preserving, it was also a valued cooking spice. Mustard, like saffron, was also home-produced. Pepper was the only spice imported in large quantities. Everyone, high and low, used a great deal of it.

Salt was vital to the medieval diet as it was the main method of preserving meat during winter. Two methods were used – dry-curing and brining. The first involved laying meat in a bed of salt, while the latter was a method whereby meat was suspended in a strong solution of salt and water. The first method gave the best results but was very hard work as the salt had to be pounded from the solid blocks into fine crystals. In important households a special servant known as the 'powderer' was employed to do this job. The vast, and often elaborately decorated, salt cellar on the table at a feast was a guide to a person's status in medieval England. If you were someone of importance you would be placed 'above the salt'.

Killing, butchering and salting a pig for winter

However, medieval people wanted more than just salt, pepper and mustard as condiments. Wealthy European cookery was aromatic and pungent with ginger, cinnamon, nutmeg, mace, cardamoms and cloves, and other spices we no longer use such as galingale, grains of paradise and cubebs. They were popular because they masked and improved the taste, not so much of tainted food (although they helped that too) but of the seemingly unending salted and dried winter foods.

These were more expensive for the British than for anyone else because they were not imported in direct shipments but had to be bought at markets on the continent of Europe. The merchants who did this obviously charged for it.

Grocers also made up and sold convenient ready-ground mixed spices to medieval housewives. The most usual mixtures were called powdor fort and powdor douce. Recipes varied, but powdor fort, which was 'hot', generally included ginger, pepper, and mace, and sometimes dried chives. Powdor douce contained ginger or cinnamon, nutmeg, sometimes cloves, a little black pepper and sugar.

We are often told that medieval cookery was thoroughly over-spiced and certainly some of it was for our tastes. But the number of spices used in a dish does not tell us how much of each was used, or their strength. Spices had been brought long distances, by sea or overland in all weather and must often have lost their original intensity of flavour by the time they arrived. Moreover, since they were so costly, they were hardly likely to be used over generously. Spicing may well have been no stronger than indicated in the following recipes.

One other interesting aspect of medieval food might surprise us now. Not only was it spiced, it was highly scented and coloured as well. Jellies were set in different coloured layers for a striped effect, rice pudding was bi-coloured, custards were reddened and

Coloured blancmanges and jellies were a great delicacy in the Middle Ages

'A cook they hadde with hem for the
    nones,
To boille the chicknes with the mary-bones,
And poudre-marchant tart, and galingale.
Wel coude he knowe a draughte of
    London ale.
He could roste, and sethe, and broille,
    and frye,
Maken mortreux, and wel bake a pye.
But greet harm was it, as thoughte me,
That on his shine a mormal hadde he;*
For blankmanger, that made he with
    the beste.'

Geoffrey Chaucer c. 1340-1400
Prologue, *Canterbury Tales*, description of the Cook

* Chaucer based his description on Roger Ware, a well-known London cook

meatballs gilded. Saffron provided yellow, sandalwood red, parsley juice green, and turnsole purple. For a particularly ostentatious gift, food was gilded with thin sheets of gold leaf.

There were times of desperate famine in the Middle Ages. The Black Death left villages depopulated, with few to till the soil or sow next year's grain. Local battles during the Wars of the Roses left the fields trampled flat, the livestock slaughtered or driven off, and the field-workers gone. The few people left grubbed roots from the ground, ate marsh plants and trapped small wild creatures to survive.

Yet, in the years between, the land was kindly and there was still a wealth of natural food plants and creatures. Medieval people's food resources were restricted, and some which could have helped them greatly (such as fresh fruits and vegetables) were largely ignored or maltreated. But even a peasant had certain customary rights to land, grazing and food which a wise lord respected, and certain things of his own, such as his cow and strip of land in the communal field.

Recipes

FLESH-DAY DISHES

BEEF OR MUTTON OLIVES

Alows de beef or de motoun: 'Take fayre Bef of the quyschons, and mouton of the bottes, and kytte in the maner of Stekys; then take raw Percely, and Oynonys smal y-scredde, and yolkys of Eyroun sothe hard, and Marow or swette, and hew alle thes to-geder smal; then caste ther-on poudere of Gyngere and Saffroun, and tolle hem to-gederys with thin hond, and lay hem on the Stekys al a-brode, and caste Salt ther-to; then rolle to-gederys, and putte hem roste hem til they ben y-now; than ley hem in a dyssche, and pore ther-on Vynegre and a lityl verious, and pouder Pepir ther-on y-now, and Gyngere, and Canelle, and a fewe yolkys of hard Eyroun y-kremyd ther-on; and serue forth.'

Today, use lamb instead of mutton, and a little extra cider vinegar instead of verjuice (sour grape or apple juice). If you wish, brush the olives with beaten egg shortly before the end of the cooking time. This was called endoring, and was often done to give spit-roasted meats a golden colour.

4 thin slices of beef topside or lamb rump

I large onion

6 hard-boiled egg yolks

Opposite: A 'marchpane' made with moulded marzipan and decorated with spun sugar

15 ml (1 tbls) shredded suet
10 ml (2 tsps) finely chopped parsley
a pinch of ground ginger
a pinch of powdered saffron
salt
a little butter
cider vinegar for sprinkling
a little ground ginger, cinnamon and black pepper mixed, for sprinkling

Beat the meat thin and flat with a cutlet bat. Chop the onion finely with 4 egg yolks. Add the suet, parsley, ginger, saffron and salt to taste. Knead and squeeze until pasty, using the onion liquid to bind. (If necessary, add a few drops of water or a little extra parsley.) Spread the stuffing on the meat slices and roll them up like small Swiss rolls. Secure with wooden toothpicks. Lay side by side in a greased baking tin, with the cut edges underneath. Dot with butter. Bake, turning once, at gas mark 4, 180° C (350° F) for 35-40 minutes. Baste once or twice while baking.

Lay the olives on a warmed serving dish. Just before serving, sprinkle with vinegar and spices, and garnish with the remaining egg yolks, crumbled.

Harleian MS 279

The vast amount of food consumed by the wealthy during the Middle Ages is well illustrated by the list of expenses recorded by the Embassy from Aragon during their two-month stay in England during 1415. There were four ambassadors and their servants and this is what they consumed on a typical day with the cost of it (although mathematics were not their strong point!).

Tuesday, 30th day of July (in London)

For white bread, 21 pence; beer, 6 pence; 20 half-flagons of wine at 4 pence each, 6 shilling 10 pence; fuel 13 pence; meat dish of pork, 13 pence; meat dish of mutton, 2 shillings 8 pence; meat dish of beef, 18 pence; 2 suckling pigs, 16 pence; 6 ducks at 3 pence, 18 pence; 4 chickens and baked pork meat dish, 3 shillings 6 pence; spices, 4 pence; plums and pears, 8 pence; Romney wine, 6 pence; meat dish of veal, 12 pence; 24 pigeons, 15 pence; 8 pullets at 2 pence, 20 pence; vinegar and mustard, 4 pence; candles, 8 pence; hay, 3 shillings 9 pence half-penny; 5 bushels oats at 8 pence, 3 shillings 4 pence; horse-bread, 3 shillings 7 pence half-penny, and for beds, 4 pence.

Total – 39 shillings 3 pence

BROILED VENISON OR BEEF STEAKS

Stekys of venson or bef: 'Take Venyson or Bef, & leche & gredyl it up broun; then take Vynegre & a litel verious, & a lytil Wyne, & putte pouder pepir ther-on y-now, and pouder Gyngere; & atte the dressoure straw on pouder Canelle y-now, that the stekys be al y-helid ther-wyth, & but a little Sawce; & than serue it forth.'

**4 trimmed venison or beef steaks,
   each weighing 175 g (6 oz)**
cooking fat (optional)
275 ml (¹/₂ pt) red wine
50 ml (2 fl oz) water
5 ml (1 tsp) brown sugar
5 ml (1 tsp) red wine vinegar
5 ml (1 tsp) lemon juice
a grinding of black pepper
a pinch of ginger
a sprinkling of cinnamon

Beat out the steaks slightly, then brush lightly with cooking fat if you wish. Heat a thick-based frying pan and sear the steaks on both sides. Reduce the heat and cook slowly until done, turning as required. Meanwhile, put all the remaining ingredients except the cinnamon in a small saucepan, and bring to the boil. Leave off the heat to infuse for 5 minutes. Sprinkle cooked steaks with cinnamon and pour a little sauce over each one before serving.

Harleian MS 279

Sweet southern French and Mediterranean wines were popular when this recipe was used. They were often thin and raw-tasting, and might be drunk watered. In this recipe, some water and sugar have been added.

BEEF AND VEGETABLE POTTAGE

Pottage was everyone's fare, at feasts and everyday meals alike. This one was called 'lange wortys de chare'.

900 g (2 lb) shin of beef
4-6 short pieces of marrow-bone
2.3 l (4 pt) water
2 leeks
2 sticks celery
2 onions
¹/₄ firm white cabbage
100 g (4 oz) 'white' breadcrumbs
a few saffron strands
10 ml (2 tsps) salt
ground black pepper

Cut the meat into 5 cm (2 in) cubes. Put in a stewpan with the bones and water. Bring to the boil and skim well. Reduce the heat, and simmer, uncovered, for about 2-2¹/₂ hours. Meanwhile, prepare the vegetables and boil in a separate pan, whole or in large pieces, for 10 minutes. Drain and cut into thick slices. When the beef is just about ready, remove the marrow-bones and add the vegetables. Continue simmering until the vegetables are soft. Stir in the breadcrumbs, saffron and plenty of seasoning. Bring back to the boil, and cook for 2-3 minutes. Skim off any excess fat before serving.

Harleian MS 279

The old recipe specifies a loaf of white bread which would have been a small, bun-like loaf made with unbleached soft wheat. A large scone round made with un-bleached (or a mixture of white and wholemeal flour) would be something like it.

STUFFED CHICKEN

Grapes, when in season, were suggested as an alternative to onions for the stuffing and sheep's fat as an alternative to lard. The bird was roasted on a simple, hand-turned spit over a wood fire (see illustration on page 74).

1.6 kg (3¹/₂ lb) chicken
4 hard-boiled eggs
2 medium onions
275 ml (¹/₂ pt) chicken stock
1 small bunch parsley
30-45 ml (2-3 tbls) lard
salt
pepper
1.5 ml (¹/₄ tsp) ground ginger
1.5 ml (¹/₄ tsp) cinnamon

Prepare the chicken for stuffing and for spit or oven roasting. Separate the egg whites and yolks. Slice the onions thinly. Bring the stock to the boil, and blanch the onions and parsley for 2-3 minutes. Remove the parsley, and cook the onions until soft. Drain, reserving the remaining stock. Cool.

Cut off the parsley stalks and chop the leaves with the egg yolks, lard, seasoning and spices. Add the onion. Stuff the chicken with the mixture, then truss it. Roast the chicken in the usual way, with the reserved stock in the drip-tray or roasting tin. Use it to baste the chicken and then to make a thin, or slightly thickened, gravy with the pan juices and some extra stock.

If wished, the chicken may be garnishished with the egg whites (chopped) and a little extra parsley, before serving.

Harleian MS 4016

GRAPE-STUFFED BOILED CHICKEN

*Chykens in hocchee: 'Take chykens
and scald them, take parsel and sawge,
with any other erbes, take garlec and
grapes, and stoppe the chickens ful, and
seeth them in good broth, so that they
may esely be boyled thereinne. Messe
them and cast thereto powdor-douce.'*

2 chickens, each 1.1 kg (2½ lb)
225 g (8 oz) green grapes
minced parsley and fresh sage
  leaves, mixed, to coat grapes
4 garlic cloves or to taste
salt and ground black pepper
850 ml (1½ pt) chicken stock
powdor douce for sprinkling (see
  note)

Prepare the birds for boiling. Halve and
seed the grapes, and coat them thickly
with the minced herbs. Chop the garlic

finely or crush it, and mix with the grapes.
Season the mixture to taste, then stuff the
birds with it. Truss the birds, enclosing the
stuffing securely. Place the birds on a thick
cloth in a stewpan. Add enough stock to
come three-quarters of the way up their
sides. Bring slowly to the boil, lower the
heat and simmer for about 45-60 minutes
until tender. Place on a warmed serving
dish and sprinkle with the powdor douce.

Mrs Groundes-Peaces's Old Cookery Notebook

For the powdor douce in this case,
mix 2.5 ml (½ tsp) each of ground
cinnamon, grated nutmeg and
ground black pepper, and 5 ml
(1 tsp) white sugar. Recipes varied,
but always included either
cinnamon or ginger.

DRESSED SWAN OR PEACOCK

The flesh of both birds was thought tough and indigestible from early times. However, one or the other was served in full plumage at most great banquets because it was so handsome. Probably, as today, a cured skin with feathers, feathered head with beak and a bunch of tail features were kept for dressing a bird each time it was needed. The bird was presented as if sitting on its nest, the head being held erect by a rod or skewer thrust through the mouth, down the throat into the breast. The swan was the most expensive (it cost 3s 4d in 1380). It was presented garlanded and crowned, on a silver or gold stand, with its wings erect, neck arched backwards, head erect, at least at royal banquets. It was much more commonly served than peacock, and is occasionally still served today. Both the Vintners' Company and the Dyers' Company hold swan-upping dinners.

Swan dight: 'Kutte a Swan in the rove of the mouthe toward the brayne enlonge, and lete him blede, and kepe the blode for chawdewyn; or elles knytte a knot on his nek, and so late his nekke breke; then skald him. Drawe him and rost him even as thou doest goce in all pyntes, and serue him forth with chawd-wyne.'

Chaudron (chawdron) was a special sauce for swans. It was made of the bird's own guts, cut small and boiled in broth with its blood and vinegar and strong spices. It looked blackish and was served hot. (Swan was quite often served as an ordinary dish, without the head.)

Pecok dight: 'Take a Pecok, breke his necke, and kutte his throte, And fle him, the skyn and the ffethurs togidre, and the hede still to the skyn of the nekke, And kepe the skyn and the ffethurs hole togiders; draw him as an hen, and kepe the bone to the necke hole, And roste him, and set the bone of the necke aboue the broche, as he was wonte to sitte a lyve, And aboue the legges to the body, as he was wonte to sitte a-lyve; And whan he is rosted ynowe, take him of, And lete him kele; And then wynde the skyn with the fethurs and the taile abought the body, And serue him forthe as he were a-live; or elles pull him dry, And roste him and serue him as thou doest a henne.'

In other words, truss in an erect position after flaying; roast, cool, then cover the skin and feathers like a jacket. Present like a swan, but with gilded comb instead of a crown, and a gold chain instead of a garland.

Harleian MS 4016

STEWED MUTTON

'Take faire Mutton that hath ben
roste, or elles Capons, or suche other
flessh, and mynce it faire; put hit
into a possenet, or elles bitwen ij
siluer disshes; caste thereto faire
parcely, And oynons small mynced;
then caste there-to wyn, and a litel
vynegre or vergeous, pouder of peper,
Canel, salt and saffron, and lete it
stue on the faire coles, And then
serue hit for the; if he have no wyne
ne vynegre, take Ale, Mustard, and
A quantite of vergeous, and do this
in the stede of vyne or vinegre.'

**About 450 g (1 lb) cold roast
   lamb**
10 ml (2 tsps) chopped parsley
1 medium onion, finely chopped
5 cm (2 in) piece cinnamon stick
salt
pepper
a pinch of saffron strands
10 ml (2 tsps) red wine vinegar
200 ml (7 fl oz) red wine

Dice or chop the meat into small
pieces, and put in a flameproof pot
or a saucepan. Add the parsley,
onion and cinnamon stick. Season
well. Sprinkle the saffron strands
over the meat, then pour over the
vinegar and wine. Bring to the boil
and cook until the onion is soft and
the meat well heated through. Add a
little extra wine if the 'stew' looks
like drying out, but do not make it
sloppy. When served, the liquid
should be almost reduced to a syrup
or glaze.

Harleian MS 4016

Add a little brown sugar or honey to the stew if you wish.

In most of the recipes it has been assumed that a kitchen-boy would have ground the spices, although it is unlikely he would have made them to the fineness we are used to. In this recipe, a piece of cinnamon stick would certainly have been used, so it has been kept.

'And therefore whoever sends you word that I have spent you any money sin ye went hence, they must give you another reckoning, saving in meat and drink, for I eat like an horse of purpose to eat you out at the doors ...'

John Paston III to John Paston II,
May 1469, *The Paston Letters*

SALAD

Salat: 'Take parsel, sawge, garlec, chibollas, oynons, leek, borage, myntes, porrectes, fenel, and ton tressis, rew, rosemarye, purslayne, lave, and waisshe hem clene. Pike hem, pluk hem small with thyn hond and myng hem wel with rawe oile. Lay on vynegar and salt and serve it forth.'

Use some or all of the following fresh vegetables and herbs:

spring onions, parsley, leeks, sage, borage, mint, fennel, garlic, watercress, rosemary, purslane

Wash the vegetables and herbs. Prepare and slice the vegetables thinly, and grate the garlic. Shred the herbs. Mix with enough olive or walnut oil to moisten. Sprinkle with vinegar and salt, and serve.

John Russell's Boke of Nurture

RASTONS

These were small round loaves or large rolls, made of sweetened bread dough enriched with eggs, like a brioche paste. After baking, the tops were cut off 'in the manner of a crown', and the crumb was removed. The crumb was finely chopped with a knife and mixed with clarified butter. It was then replaced in the hollowed bread crusts. The tops were replaced and the loaves or rolls were returned to the oven for a few moments to heat through.

Small rolls are more practical for modern meals. Make a brioche paste, and bake it in deep bun tins. When baked, cut off the tops, remove the crumb and mix with just enough clarified butter to moisten. Replace the tops and return to the oven for 5-7 minutes. Serve hot.

Harleian MS 279

LENTEN AND FISH-DAY DISHES

HOT WINE BEVERAGE

A caudle was a hot wine drink thickened with eggs, which was drunk at breakfast or bedtime. This was a version for Lent or Fridays when, strictly, eggs were not allowed.

275 ml ('/2 pt) water
850 ml (1 '/2 pt) white wine
225 g (8 oz) ground almonds
2.5 ml ('/2 tsp) ground ginger
5 ml (1 tsp) clear honey or
**   white sugar**
a good pinch of salt
a good pinch of powdered
**   saffron or a few drops of**
**   yellow food colouring**

Assessing the quality of the wine

Bring the water and wine to the boil in a saucepan. Tip in the almonds, and add the ginger, honey or sugar and salt. Stir in the saffron or food colouring, and leave off the heat to steep for 15-30 minutes. Bring back to the boil, and serve very hot, in small heatproof bowls.

The Forme of Cury

LENTEN STEW

'Soupes dorroy' was listed as a pottage (soup-stew), so the original recipe can be interpreted as either a soup or a semi-solid main dish for my lord's Lenten dinner, depending on how much liquid is used. From the way it is written this version of the recipe (there are several) seems to be a main dish.

8 large onions
125 ml (4 fl oz) sunflower oil for frying
100 g (4 oz) ground almonds
2.5 ml (^{1}/$_2$ tsp) honey
a pinch of salt
150 ml (^{1}/$_4$ pt) boiling water
150 ml (^{1}/$_4$ pt) white wine
8 rounds of 'white' bread or brioche, crusts removed, about 3 cm (1^1/$_4$ in) thick

Slice the onions into rings, and simmer them in the oil, turning often, until soft and golden. Leave aside in the pan. Put the almonds in a small saucepan. Mix the honey and salt into the water, and pour it over the almonds with half the wine. Leave to soak for 10 minutes, stirring occasionally. Meanwhile toast the bread lightly on both sides. Lay the slices side by side in a shallow dish. Add the remaining wine to the onions, and simmer until they are reheated through. Heat the almond milk until steaming and pour it over the toast slices. Pile onions on top.

Harleian MS 279

ALMOND MILK

'Cold milk of almondes' was a basic ingredient used as a fast-day substitute for other thickened liquids in many medieval dishes. Only one recipe is known, dated about 1467; it is quoted by Lorna Sass in her book *To the King's Taste* and is for thick almond milk served cold. Modern ground almonds make a slightly gritty liquid; grinding in a blender before use helps, but do not let them 'oil'. Use the following proportions:

50 g (2 oz) almonds, blanched, skinned and ground

For thin milk:
2.5 ml (¹/₂ tsp) honey or white sugar
a good pinch of salt
200 ml (7 fl oz) boiling water
30 ml (2 tbls) white wine

For thick milk (like coating white sauce):
1.5 ml (¹/₄ tsp) honey or white sugar
a good pinch of salt
65 ml (2¹/₂ fl oz) boiling water
15 ml (1 tbls) white wine

Put the almonds in a bowl. Add the honey or sugar and salt to the water, and pour over the almonds. Leave to stand for 15-30 minutes, stirring occasionally. Mix in the wine. Strain thin milk if a particular recipe requires it. Refrigerate in a covered container for up to 48 hours.

The original recipe suggests boiling the water with the sweetening and salt, one suspects to a syrup – indicating that the medieval palate liked its sauces sweetened much more heavily than above. Add extra honey or sugar to dessert dishes.

COOKING SUNDRY FISH

Floundres boiled: 'Take floundres and drawe hem in the side by the hede [gut through a slit below the head] . . . and make sauce of water and salt and a good quantite of ale; and whan hit biginneth to boile, skeme it, and caste hem there-to; And late hem sethe [boil]; and serue hem forth hote; and no sauce but salt, or as a man luste.'

Shrympes: 'Take shrympes, and seth hem in water and a litull salt, and lete hem boil ones or a litull more. And serue hem forthe colde; And no maner sauce but vinegre.'

Sole, boiled . . . or fryed: 'Take a sole and do away the hede, and drawe him as a plais [plaice – or flounder, see above] and fle [skin] him; and make sauce of water, parcelly and salt; And whan hit bygynneth to boile, skeme it clene, and lete boyle ynogh. And if thoy wilt haue him in sauce, take hime whan he is y-sodde [add it after boiling] . . . Or elles take a sole, and do away the hede; draw him, and scalde him, and pryk him with a knyfe in diuerse [various] place for brekyng of the skin [to prevent curling]; And fry it in oyle, or elles in pured [clarified] buttur.'

Follow modern cooking methods, i.e. simmer or poach the fish, rather than boiling furiously. There is no need to skim impurities off modern salt, tap-water and beer.

Harleian MS 4016

PIKE WITH GALENTYNE SAUCE

You can boil the pike (in ale and water) as in the old recipe if you wish, but sousing it helps to dissolve the little hair-bones which are such a trial to eat. The method was well known at this period. Galentyne sauce was strongly flavoured and more like a condiment. There were several versions of it; the one here is the version in the original recipe for pike except that sandalwood has been omitted. This recipe is for cold fish with hot sauce. Another version, which follows it closely, is for hot fish smothered in (stronger-flavoured) cold sauce. Lampreys were also served with sauce galentyne as dressing, and fillets of roast pork were served in a thickened spiced red wine sauce also called galentyne.

1.4 kg (3 lb) middle cut pike
700 ml (1 1/4 pt) malt vinegar
1/2 small carton pickling spice
4 bay leaves

For the sauce:
75 g (3 oz) dark rye breadcrumbs
60 ml (4 tbls) white wine
45-60 ml (3-4 tbls) water
30 ml (2 tbls) white wine vinegar
1.5 ml (1/4 tsp) cinnamon
salt and ground black pepper
30 ml (2 tbls) grated onion
10 ml (2 tsps) sunflower oil

Put the fish in a non-metallic ovenproof dish and pour the malt vinegar over it. Add enough water to three-quarters cover the fish, and include the spice and bay leaves. Cover, and soak for 24-48 hours in a cool place. Then put in the oven at gas mark 2, 150° C (300° F) and cook for 2-2½ hours. Cool in the liquid, then drain and skin. To make the sauce, put the breadcrumbs in a bowl. Add the wine, water and vinegar, and sprinkle with the spice and seasonings. Leave for 1-2 hours to soften. Meanwhile, simmer the onion in the oil until soft. Mash the bread sauce until pasty, adding a little extra water if over strong or too solid. Stir in the fried onion. Put in a small saucepan, and bring to the boil. Pour over the cold fish just before serving.

Harleian MS 4016

Substitute middle-cut cod for the pike, if you prefer.

Medieval wines were often sweetened – if the completed sauce is too sharp, add a little sugar.

SAUCE VERT

'*Take percely, myntes, diteyne, peletre, a foil or ij of cost marye, a cloue of garleke. And take faire brede, and stepe it with vynegre and piper, and salt; and grynde al this to-gedre, and tempre it up with wynegre, or with eisel, and serue it forth.*'

This was a very popular type of sauce in medieval times because it masked the taste of fish which was slightly 'off', over-salted or just muddy. Mint sauce is almost the only modern survivor. Dittany, pellitory, and costmary had almost 'gone out' by the end of Tudor times, when more pleasing herbs had come into use. Use any fresh herbs you can get, the more the better.

Suggested proportions:

Leaves of 10–12 sprigs parsley, mint and other fresh herbs

1 garlic clove

50 g (2 oz) fine 'white' breadcrumbs

30 ml (2 tbls) cider vinegar

salt

freshly ground black pepper

wine vinegar and/or water as needed

Chop the herbs finely. Parsley and mint should predominate. Squeeze the garlic over the herbs in a mortar. Sprinkle the breadcrumbs with the cider vinegar and leave for 10 minutes. Add to the herbs with salt and pepper. Pound until well blended. Then add enough wine vinegar or water, or a mixture, to give you a consistency rather like thickened mint sauce (or green bread sauce). Serve with broiled or poached fish.

Ashmole MS 1439

Mint (left) and sage were used to flavour many dishes

DRIED PEA PURÉE WITH SPROUTS

The original recipe describes how to hull the dried peas by soaking them in boiling wine lees and water overnight, then rubbing them in a cloth and rinsing. This shortened the boiling time. The recipe below adapts the method for modern hulled peas. Also, since bean sprouts are easier to buy than pea sprouts, they have been used as a substitute for the sprouted peas in the original recipe.

625 g (1¹/₄ lb) white or yellow peas
700 ml (1 bottle) white wine
salt
1 carton bean sprouts
pepper

Soak the peas in the wine overnight, with water to cover if needed. Simmer in the same liquid, with a little salt, for 2-2¹/₂ hours or until mushy, adding extra water if needed. (There should be almost no free liquid at the end, and the peas should be reduced to a purée.)

Add the bean sprouts, stir in and simmer until tender. Season with salt and pepper before serving.

Harleian MS 279

BUTTERED VEGETABLES

Buttered wortes: 'Take all maner of good herbes that through may gete, and do bi ham as is forsaid; putte hem on the fire with faire water; put there-to clarified buttur a grete quantite. Whan thei ben boyled ynogh, salt hem; late none otemele come there-in. Dise brede small in disshes, and powre on the wortes, and serue hem forth.'

700 g (1 ¹/₂ lb) mixed fresh vegetables
50 g (2 oz) clarified butter
2 slices 'white' or wholemeal bread, crusts removed
salt
pepper

Prepare the vegetables and chop or slice them neatly, keeping separate any which need only a short cooking time. Put the rest into a saucepan with just enough water to come halfway up the vegetables, and the butter. Bring to the boil, cover, lower the heat and cook gently until tender. Add the short-cooking vegetables partway through the cooking time. Add extra boiling water during cooking if needed to prevent the vegetables drying out. Cut the bread slices into small cubes or dice and put them in a heated vegetable dish. Season vegetables to taste, and turn them into the dish on top of the bread. Dot with extra butter if you wish.

Harleian MS 4016

PEAS AND ONIONS WITH SIPPETS

The old recipe suggests green or white peas as alternatives. Other recipes indicate that green peas meant fresh peas as today, and that white peas were dried ones for winter use.

900 g (2 lb) shelled fresh peas
3 medium onions
5 sprigs parsley (leaves only)
2 sage leaves, finely chopped
a good grinding of black pepper
30 ml (2 tbls) white wine
30 ml (2 tbls) white wine vinegar
a pinch of powdered saffron
salt to taste
4 slices 'white' bread, crusts
  removed and diced

Cook the peas in plenty of water (but no salt) until tender. Strain off 275 ml (½ pint) of the cooking water into a clean pan. Drain the peas and keep warm. Chop the onions and parsley finely, and add to the reserved cooking liquid, with the sage and pepper. Add the wine. Bring to the boil, and add all the remaining ingredients except the bread. Boil down to half the original quantity, or slightly less. Mix in the peas, then bread dice. Reheat if necessary, then serve.

Ancient Cookery

Herbs were grown for medicinal use as well as for cookery. Comfrey was used for fractures, feverfew for migraines, wormwood for intestinal worms and mugwort to fend off evil spirts

Garlic and herb mixtures as used by medieval apothecaries

LOSYNS (LOZENGES)

'Take a good broth and do in an erthen pot. Take flour of pandemayn and therof past with water, and make therof thynne foyles as paper with a roller; drye it harde and seeth it in brith. Take chese ruayn grated and lay it in dishes with powder douce, and lay theron loseyns isode as hoole as thou yght, and above powdour and chese; and so twyse or thryse, and serie it forth.'

150–275 ml ('/4–'/2 pt)water
2 300 g (10'/2 oz) cans beef broth
2 cans water
470 g (1 lb) cheese (hard or soft)

Stir the water into the flour and knead until smooth and elastic. Divide into four portions, roll out each to about 30cm (12in) radius. Cut into diamonds (lozenges), leave to dry. Grate the cheese and mix up the powdor douce (see page 41). Bring broth to the boil, put in pasta and cook for 10-12 minutes and drain. Put one-third of the grated cheese in a dish, sprinkle on a third of the powdor douce, then put a third of the hot pasta on top. Repeat this twice, leaving a little of powdor douce to spread on the top.

The Forme of Cury

There was great excitement in 2003 when some British newspapers reported that lasagne had, in fact, been invented in England and not Italy! This dish was cited as the proof! However, the claim was hotly denied and the Italians won the day.

You can also use a soft cheese such as mozzarella for this recipe.

SWEET DISHES

HONEY TOAST WITH PINE NUTS

'Pokerounce' make a change from the better-known similar dish called Poor Knights and are a lot less rich, being fat free and made with pure honey. The pepper – galingale in the original recipe – just takes off any cloying sweetness the honey may have.

225 g (8 oz) stiff honey

a pinch of ground ginger

a pinch of cinnamon

a pinch of ground black pepper

4 large square slices white bread, crusts removed, 10 mm (¹/₂ in) thick

15 g (¹/₂ oz) pine nut kernels

Put the honey, spices and pepper in a small saucepan over very low heat. Melt the honey and simmer for not more than 2 minutes. Do not let the honey boil or darken, or it will 'toffee'. Let it cool slightly. Meanwhile, toast the bread lightly on both sides. Cut each slice into four small squares or rectangles. Place on a heated serving plate and pour the syrupy honey over them. Then stick pine nut kernels upright in each piece, like small stakes. Serve quickly, while still hot, and eat with a knife and fork.

Harleian MS 279

'I send you 5s to buy with sugar and dates for me. I would have 3 or 4lb of sugar, and beware the remnant in dates, and send them to me as hastily as ye may. And send me word what price a pound of pepper, cloves, maces, ginger, cinnamon, almonds, rice, raisins of currants, galingale, saffron, grains, and comfits – of each of these send me word what a pound is worth, and if it be better cheap at London than it is here I shall send you money to buy such stuff as I will have ...'

Margaret Paston to John Paston III,
5th November 1471, *The Paston Letters*

DATE SLICES WITH SPICED WINE

There are several old versions of this favourite medieval recipe – 'leche lumbard'. This one makes an excellent (and healthful) sweetmeat for modern use, because it keeps for 2–3 weeks in a refrigerator if left unsliced.

800 g (1¾ lb) stoneless block dates
425 ml (¾ pt) medium-dry white wine
75 g (3 oz) light soft brown sugar
2.5 ml (½ tsp) cinnamon
2.5 ml (½ tsp) ground ginger
6 hard-boiled egg yolks
about 150 g (6 oz) soft brown breadcrumbs (not wholemeal)
45–60 ml (3–4 tbls) Madeira heated with a pinch of mixed spice

Break up the dates and simmer with the wine and sugar until pulpy. Pound or put through a food processor until almost smooth. Mix in the spices and sieve or work in the egg yolks. In a bowl, knead in enough breadcrumbs to make the mixture as stiff as marzipan. Form it into a 5 cm (2 in) diameter roll, and chill until firm. Cut into 5mm (¼ in) slices. Arrange in overlapping lines on a plate, and trickle a drop or two of cooled, spiced wine over each slice.

Harleian MS 4016

PEARS IN WINE SYRUP

This is one of the earliest of many recipes for 'warduns in syruppe'. It suggests mulberries as red fruit, but loganberries make a good modern substitute. It also suggests 'wyn crete or vernage' for the syrup; this usually meant a sweet southern Italian or Cypriot white wine or one from Tuscany. Wardens were a large type of pear.

3 large firm dessert pears
298 g (10 oz) can mulberries or loganberries
275 ml ('/2 pt) full-flavoured red wine
a few drops of red food colouring
150 ml ('/4 pt) sweet white Italian wine
25 g (1 oz) white sugar
a good pinch of ground ginger
a small pinch of cinnamon
a small pinch of ground black pepper

Peel the pears but leave them whole. Gouge out the hard cores from the round end if you wish. Drain the berries. Put the pears and berries in a saucepan, and pour the red wine over them with a few drops of colouring. Simmer the fruit until the pears are tender, turning them often to colour them pink evenly. Cool in the liquid, turning them from time to time to deepen the colour. Drain, reserving the liquid. Cut the pears into halves or into quarters if you wish. Sieve the soft fruit and return to the pan with the cooking liquid. Put the white wine, sugar and spices in a clean pan. Boil to 105° C (215° F) or until you have a fairly thick syrup which will glaze the fruit. Add the pears, bring back to the boil, and cook for 2-3 minutes. Serve hot, with the warmed sieved fruit and red wine as a sauce.

Ancient Cookery

The original recipe specifies powdor douce to flavour the syrup. The sugar, ginger and cinnamon mixture is here based on a Tudor recipe which used 50 g (2 oz) sugar, 7 g (¹/4 oz) ginger and 3.5 g (¹/8 oz) cinnamon.

Dinner in the 15th century. The cup-bearer approaches the lady of the house and, under the balcony, the steward keeps an eye on the household servants

GINGERBREAD

'Take goode honey & clarifie it on the fere, & take fayre paynemayn or wastel brede & grate it, & caste it into the boylenge hony, & stere it will togydr faste with a sklse that bren not to the vessell. & thanne take it doun and put thein ginger, long pepere & saundres, & tempere it up with thin handel; & than put hem to a flatt boyste & strawe theron suger, & pick therin clowes round about by the egge and in the myudes yf it plece you &c.'

Place honey in a small saucepan and bring to the boil on a low heat. Skim off the scum that forms on the top of the honey. Stir in the breadcrumbs then remove from the heat. Mix in the spices and place the mixture in a Swiss roll tin. Cut into pieces when cold and serve decorated with whole cloves (optional).

Harleian MS 4016

575 ml (I pint) honey
435 g (15 oz) breadcrumbs
25 ml (5 tsp) ground ginger
5 ml (I tsp) pepper
5 ml (I tsp) ground sandalwood
cloves

SWEET CHEESE FLAN

*Tart de bry: 'Take a croste ynch depe
in trape. Take zolkes of ayren rawe
and chese ruayn. Medle it and
zolkes togyd and do ther-to poudor,
gynger, sugar, saffron and salt. Do it
in a trape, bak it and serve it forth.'*

The costly medieval sugar came in
close-packed loaves, whitish outside
with treacly residues in the centre.
The wealthy had whitish sugar cut
or scraped off the loaf but in
coarser grains than granulated
sugar. Caster sugar is
recommended, however, for a
lighter cheesecake.

'Chese ruayn' meant any rich
soft cheese. Brie was well known in
England but must have been costly.
Anne Wilson therefore suggests that
it was almost certainly made up

with local ruayn or rewain cheese,
as the old recipe recommends.

**Shortcrust pastry made with
150 g (5 oz) flour and 65 g
(2¹/₂ oz) lard**

a pinch of powdered saffron
15 ml (1 tbls) very hot water
**350 g (12 oz) Brie cheese,
without rind, or full fat soft
cheese**
4 egg yolks
50 g (2 oz) caster sugar
a good pinch of ground ginger
a pinch of salt

Use the pastry to line an 20 cm (8 in)
flan case. Steep the saffron powder in
the water until the liquid is deep gold.
Meanwhile, beat the cheese until
creamy and quite smooth. In a separate

bowl, beat the egg yolks and sugar together until thick and pale. Beat in the softened cheese little by little, then the ginger, salt and saffron water. Turn the mixture into the prepared case. Bake at gas mark 5, 190° C (375° F) for 20–25 minutes or until just set in the centre. Serve warm or cold the same day.

The Forme of Cury

The effigy on the tomb of a great medieval chef called Taillevent bears a coat of arms displaying three cooking pots

CURD FLAN

Lese fryes: 'Take nessh chese, and pare it clene, and grinde hit in a morter small, and drawe yolkes and white of egges thorgh a streynour, and cast there-to, and grinde hem togidre; then cast thereto Sugur, butter and salt, and put al togidre in a coffyn of faire paast, and lete bake ynowe, and then serue it forth.'

This is similar to the previous recipe except that it is made with 'nessh' (fresh soft curd) cheese. Note the neat method of blending and liquifying the egg whites and yolks by straining them.

Use the cheese flan recipe, using smooth curd (not cottage) cheese with 30 ml (2 tbls) butter and 2 large or 3 small eggs. Omit the ginger and saffron.

Harleian MS 4016

69

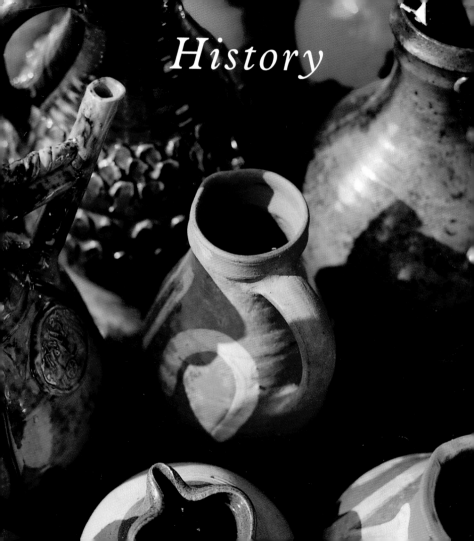

COOKING METHODS AND TOOLS

Cooking methods depend on cooking facilities. A rural cottager, whether free, tenant or serf, had only a one-room home with a fire built on a large flat stone in the centre, or against a wall if his hut had stone walls; the embers would keep the 'down-hearth' stone fairly hot. If a beam stretched across the hut, the housewife might have a cast-iron cauldron hanging from it; but she was more likely to use earthenware pots standing in the hot ashes beside the fire, or balanced on a tall stone among the embers.

She could seethe (boil) her pottage in this way, stirring it with a ladle or spurtle (wooden stick). But if she wanted to bake, she needed more equipment. Although the manorial lord demanded that his peasants should get their corn ground by his licensed miller for a fee, it was hard to enforce, and many people ground their small quantity of grain in a hardwood mortar, stone trough or in a hand-quern; they mixed it with water and baked their unleavened bread or oatcakes on the down-hearth under an upturned pot.

Opposite: A selection of pottery in medieval styles

Instead of roasting, small birds, hedgehogs or a poached squirrel might be wrapped in clay and baked in the hottest ashes, as might fresh fish, but salt herring was best boiled.

A village tradesman or artisan lived almost as simply but his home would probably have had two rooms or at least partitions, with the fire in the living area. On each side of the down-hearth, there might be iron firedogs with hooked tops to support an iron rod from which a cauldron could be hung. Whereas the poor housewife would be lucky to have two or three pottery or wooden bowls to set her milk in for cream or cheese, and probably churned her butter by hand, her grander neighbour who kept a cow might well have a new-style plunger churn worked like a pestle and mortar with a lid.

The kitchen of a castle, manor house or monastery was generally stone-floored and walled, with great wide fireplaces where most of the cooking was done. Roasting, all done on spits, might take place here, or in a separate building because of the size of the fire needed to roast all the meat required, and the risk of conflagration. The king's new separate kitchens at Clarendon in 1206 each had fires which could roast two or three whole oxen.

Roasting spits were still simple, propped on firedogs and turned by apprentice cooks or kitchen-boys. There were no women cooks or kitchen maids yet. Boy scullions cleaned the spits, basting ladles and the brushes and bowls used for applying egg-wash to gild the near-roasted joints. They lived in the kitchen and even

The kitchen fireplace in the keep of Carlisle Castle, Cumbria

slept on its floor. Scullions did not penetrate the other rooms of the kitchen complex. There were larders, storerooms and cellars, and between the kitchen and dining hall as a rule, a buttery where drink was stored and a pantry, from where bread, trenchers and salt were served.

The bakehouse was usually a separate building, with ovens built out from the walls. Wood, peat or furze was lit in the oven and left

A pair of kitchen-boys turn a roasting spit in a medieval kitchen

to burn until the interior was hot enough. The spent fuel was then quickly drawn out, the floor of the oven was cleaned, and the bread was put in to bake, along with pies, tarts and enriched breads like pastries. Long-handled rakes were used to deal with fuel and ash, while flat hardwood peels were used to lift the loaves in and out of the ovens.

The dairy was another separate structure. Here, shallow panshons (wide earthern vessels) stood to hold the milk and ladles, skimmers, jugs and brushes hung on the walls. A heavy cheese-press would stand in a corner with a tall churn beside it, and perhaps the dairymaid's pails and yoke.

Back in the main kitchen, the only large pieces of furniture were the heavy table used as a work-surface, where pottage vegetables were cut up, and the chopping block for meat joints. Boiling was done in cauldrons hooked on to pot-hangers over the fire. Other pots and pans, usually of heavy metal with long handles, could be held over the

'Seal' jugs, named after the circular applied discs on the shoulders, were in use from the late 12th century onwards

fire for making sauces or boiling eggs. There were also flatter, long-handled pans like our frying pans, and used for the same purposes.

The professional medieval cook had two other cooking appliances. One was a grid of metal bars on a long handle, on which food could be broiled over the fire (instead of under it like a modern grill). The other resembled a two sided waffle-iron, and was used to make crisp batter wafers.

He had, of course, other kitchen tools: cleavers, knives and mallets, special tongs for cutting sugar, bunches of twigs for whisking and scouring, pestles and mortars of all sizes and weights, to name just a few. Plus cloths, scouring sand and tubs for washing up!

Cooking over an open fire with 16th-century style cooking pots

TABLE SERVICE AND ETIQUETTE

The way the usual two-course dinner was conducted in a 14th- or early 15th-century manorial household was important to everyone who took part. Whether he was serving or sat in the lowest seat, it showed that he had a rightful, allotted place in this intricate social work hierarchy, with both duties and customary rights.

Every day, when at home, the lords of the manor dined with his household in the Great Hall. It was always a formal meal to some degree, to show his own status, but he would generally hear requests and complaints before or afterwards as well as hand out the odd favour or rebuke. It helped everyone to know more or less where he stood.

How well this worked depended on the lord's status. The king or an archbishop dined in state every day, and only great nobles or prelates could get near them; but a good lesser lord was usually approachable, except at a feast, which was mainly an occasion for display and entertainment.

We know much more about medieval feasts, especially grand ones, than about ordinary dinners, because the method of serving, the seating arrangements and the menus of some of them were recorded in detail at the time, but the general plan of ordinary meals was the same, although the procedures were simplified.

At one end of the long hall was a raised platform or dais, on which the lord, his family and his frequent visitors were seated. They were placed along one side of the table, facing the room and the musicians' gallery at its other end. The lord sat in the centre (under a canopy at a feast). In the body of the hall, tables were set along its length on both sides, to seat the household and lesser guests in order of rank. The table nearest the dais, on the lord's right, was the most senior, and was called the 'Rewarde' because it was served with the dishes from the lord's own table. The table opposite it was called the 'Second Messe', and the rest

The ground-floor plan of the Great Hall of Penshurst Place in Kent, showing the site of the early medieval fire in the centre, the dais where the lord sat and the buttery and pantry

Following pages: Reconstruction drawing by Terry Ball of a high table feast taking place in Arthur's Hall at Dover Castle, Kent

79

were graded similarly (at a big feast, the lesser guests might spill over into several rooms, and even the gallery).

Under the gallery, behind screens, there were doors leading to the kitchen, buttery, cellar and pantry and near them were serving tables called cubberdes (cupboards). At one side, or in an adjoining room, there was an ewery with basins for hand-washing before the meal.

There were a few regular items on the menu which everyone used, such as trencher bread, but apart from those, there had to be different dishes for each table in the hall, and more for the top tables than others. Then, at least once a week, most of the dishes had to be chosen to exclude meat (including meat-thickened sauces) and, since both raw and cooked meat might 'go off' between Thursday and Sunday, butchering had to be carefully planned to leave as few leftovers as possible on Thursday night.

There were also special groups of people to be fed. Medical teaching of the time stated that young children should have a quite different diet from adults (excluding red meat and fruit, but including milk). Their nurse, who ate with them, ranked above most female servants. There were also the lord's almoner, secretary

This is the list of provisions required for a magnificent banquet made for King Richard II at the Bishop of Durham's Palace in London on 23rd September 1387

Xiiij (14) *oxen lying in salte*

II (2) *oxen ffreyssh*

Vi XX (120) *hedes of shepe fressh*

Vi XX (120) *carcas of shepe fressh*

Xij (12) *Bores*

Xiiij (14) *Calvys*

Cxl (140) *pigges*

CCC (300) *maribones*

Of larde and grece, ynogh

IIƷ (3) *ton of salt veneson*

IIƷ (3) *does of ffressh veneson*

L (50) *Swannes*

CCx (110) *Gees*

L (50) *capons of hie grece*

Viii dussen (96) *other capons*

Lx dd (dozen) (720) *Hennes*

CC copull (400) *Conyngges*

IIIƷ (4) *Fesauntes*

V (5) *Herons and Bitores*

VI (6) *kiddes*

V disson (dozen) (60) *pullayn for Gely*

Xii dd (dozen) (144) *to roste*

Cdd (dozen) (1,200) *pejons*

Xij dd. (dozen) (144) *partrych*

Viiij dd. (dozen) (72) *Rabettes*

X disen Curlewes

Xij. (144) *dosen Brewes*

Xij (12) *Cranes*

Wilde fowle ynogh

VI xx (six score) (120) *galons melke*

Xij galons (12) *Crème*

Xi (11) *galons of Cruddes (curds)*

Iij (3) *bushels of Appelles*

Xj thousand (11,000) *eggs*

and accountant, who were all clerics. Then, even in a modest manor, there were several other groups, there had to be a wholly separate one for the clergy.

Any menu was served in two main courses, with a dessert course afterwards for special guests at a feast. Each course consisted of a number of poultry and meat (or fish) dishes and two or three sweet ones. They were handed round to those at the high table but were put on the other tables for people to help themselves. Each dish was portioned beforehand and two or four

'She leet no morsel from hir lippes falle,
Ne wette hir fingres in hir sauce depe.
Wel coude she carie a morsel, and wel kepe,
That no drope ne fille up-on hire brest.
In curteisye was set ful muche hir lest.'

Geoffrey Chaucer, *c.*1340-1400, *Prologue, Canterbury Tales*,
description of the Prioress

people shared a portion or 'messe', either eating it from the shared platter or transferring bits to their trenchers. Sometimes cups were shared too.

A feast might have three courses and had special treats included because at the end of each course, a 'sotelte' (a carved hard-sugar sculpture relevant to the occasion) was presented to the high table. Everyone had a good look at it and, if it were edible, might get a taste. Then, when the table had been relaid for the second course, there might be a procession to bring in a decorated peacock or swan. Later the host would give presents to his main guests and there would be drinks and diversions – a jester and mummers.

The highest-ranking nobles had a steward, who ran the household. Under him the chief official at dinner was the marshal. Next in rank, in charge of different aspects of the meal, were the sewer (head waiter and taster), the pantler or panter (head of the pantry), the butler (in charge of drinks), the ewerer (in charge of hand-washing and linen), the chief cook, the carver and the lord's cup-bearer. All these except the last two had several grooms (trained staff), and underlings to help them: there were waiters, and assistant waiters who brought the food only as far as the hall; assistant cooks, their scullions and spit-boys; pot-boys and bottle-washers.

At a great English state feast, the duties of the major household officials were carried out by noblemen who would be rewarded with generous gifts – for instance the king's cup-bearer and taster might be given the solid gold cup he tasted from.

The everyday household officials always laid the tables. First, the senior ewerer laid two or three cloths on the high table and all the other tables, and set out a cloth at the ewery, a special basin for the lord and a cup from which to taste the water in it. Next, the pantler brought the lord's bread rolls wrapped in a napkin, his trenchers and the large ceremonial covered salt-cellar, together with special knives for cutting the bread, and a spoon. He laid each in a special spot in front of his master's place, this done, he saw that the other tables were provided with bread, trenchers, knives, spoons, and with trenchers for salt.

When the cooks were ready, the company assembled, but only the lord sat down as yet. Everyone else went off to wash – the sewer, carver and cup-bearer going first. These three were then equipped with towels and napkins, elaborately draped over one shoulder, and then the assay or tasting ritual took place.

Advancing towards his master with three bows, the carver went down on his knees, uncovered and moved the salt, unwrapped the lord's bread, and cut a small cornet (cone) of both white and trencher bread for the pantler to taste. At the same time, the marshal and cup-bearer advanced with the lord's hand-washing basin, tasted the water and kissed the towel he should use. The first course of dishes were by this time on the serving tables, and the sewer attacked them, giving the chief cook and the lord's chief steward a taste of them all. Every dish was marginally mutilated for fear of poison.

The carver at work on a nobleman's dinner in 1415.
From the *Book of Hours* of the Duke of Berry

'I love no roast but a nutbrown toast,
And a crab laid in the fire;
A little bread shall do me stead,
Much bread I not desire.
No frost nor snow, no wind, I trow,
Can hurt me if I would,
I am so wrapt, and thoroughly lapt
Of jolly good ale and old.

CHORUS
Back and side go bare, go bare,
Both foot and hand go cold;
But, belly, God send thee good ale enough,
Whether it be new or old.'

Anon, *A Song of Ale*, 16th century

Once these tastings were done, lesser guests sat down and the carver came to the fore. There were elaborate medieval instructions for dressing and carving the various meats and birds, and each creature was handled differently, a skilled carver priding himself on the speed and dexterity of his performance. Once he had completed his task, the first course could at last be served.

Only one thing remained to be tasted, and that was the drink. This was the job of the marshal, butler and cup-bearer and was performed with the same flourishes as the food tastings. The tasting and serving of the ale (and wine for senior ranks) was timed to coincide with the service of the first roast.

It was perhaps as well that senior officials had tasted so many dishes, because they now had to remain on their feet throughout the meal, making sure that each dish was served with the right sauce,

The Royal Gold Cup which was made in France in the 14th century and later brought to England, where it formed part of the English royal treasure

89

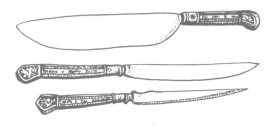

A 15th-century carving knife and two table knives. The pointed blades were used to lift food to the mouth before forks became fashionable

that everyone was served properly and that no important guest was left with an empty cup or a soiled trencher.

Then, when the meal was ended, the tables were cleared, and if the lord had guests, sweet wine was served, with perhaps wafers and whole spices as dessert. Finally grace was said, and the lord got on his feet to drink a toast as a signal that dinner was over, after which everyone went off, back to work.

Medieval table manners were carefully described in etiquette books for young people. Most of the precepts concerned personal cleanliness and how to share one's 'messe' courteously with one's neighbour. The student is told to have clean nails, and not to leave fingermarks on the table. He must not drink from a shared cup with his mouth full lest he soil it, nor drink his soup noisily. Neither must he pick his teeth with his knife, blow on his food to cool it, or wipe his mouth on the tablecloth. For his neighbour's sake, he should clean his spoon properly, nor leave it in the dish (there were no forks in those days). He should not dip his fingers too deep in the shared dish, nor crumble bread into it in case his hands were sweaty. He should definitely not gnaw bones, nor tear meat to bits with his teeth or fingers. Scratching his head at table was unacceptable, and there were other specific instructions about spitting and belching.

These basic directions seem a curious contrast to the fanciful etiquette of preparing the table, tasting and serving. But even a manorial household or similar group still consisted largely of people with a peasant and farming background; even lordlings had been brought up in close contact with peasant life and ways, in which there were no facilities for courteous living.

Pyke not thine Eris ne thy nostrellis:
If thou do, men wolle sey thou come of cherlis

Anon, *The Little Children's Little Book*, c.1480

In teaching them manners, it is significant that cleanliness and courtesy were considered priorities for both the enjoyment of food and for communal living generally. So much so that the instructions were laboriously written down by hand for generations of lords and ladies in the making to learn.

BIBLIOGRAPHY

Anon, *Ancient Cookery*, *c.*1381. In *Antiquitates Culinariae*, Richard Warner, 1791, facsimile edition by Prospect Books (London, 1983).

Anon, Ashmole MS 1439, *c.*1430. In Austin (ed.), *Two Fifteenth Century Cookery Books*, Early English Text Society, Oxford University Press (Oxford, 1964).

Anon, *The Forme of Cury*, *c.*1390. In *Antiquitates Culinariae*, Richard Warner, 1791, facsmile edition by Prospect Books (London, 1983).

Anon, Harleian MSS 279, *c.*1430 and 4016, *c.*1450. In Austin (ed.), *Two Fifteenth Century Cookery Books*, Early English Text Society, Oxford University Press (Oxford, 1964).

Braudel, Fernand, *The Structures of Everyday Life*, translated by Sian Reynolds, Collins (London, 1983).

Brett, Gerard, *Dinner is Served*, Rupert Hart Davis (London, 1968).

Buxton, Moira, *Mediaeval Cooking Today*, Kylin Press (Waddesdon, 1983).

Clair, Colin, *Kitchen and Table*, Abelard Schuman (New York, 1964).

Field, Rachael, *Irons in the Fire*, Crowood Press (Marlborough, 1984).

Harrison, Molly, *The Kitchen in History*, Osprey (London, 1972).

Horsler, Val, *Living in the Past*, Weidenfeld and Nicolson (London, 2003).

John Russell's Boke of Nurture, *c.*1460. In F. J. Furnivall (ed.), *Early English Meals and Manners*, Early English Text Society (1868).

Layton, T. A., *Five to a Feast*, Duckworth (London, 1946).

Mead, W. E., *The English Mediaeval Feast*, George Allen and Unwin (London, 1967).

Mrs Groundes-Peaces's Old Cookery Notebook, R. Howe (ed.), Rainbird Reference Books with David and Charles (Newton Abbot, 1971).

Sass, Lorna J., *To the King's Taste*, Metropolitan Museum of Art (New York, 1975).

Tannahill, Reay, *Food in History*, Eyre Methuen (London, 1973).

Wildeblood, Joan, and Brinson, Peter, *The Polite World*, Oxford University Press (Oxford, 1965).

Wilson, C. Anne, *Food and Drink in Britain*, Constable (London 1973); Penguin Books (Harmondsworth, 1984).

ACKNOWLEDGEMENTS

The publishers would like to thank Historic Haut Cuisine for cooking and presenting a number of recipes featured in this book, and James O. Davies and Peter Williams for photographing them. They also acknowledge the assistance given by Derry Brabbs in supplying photographs from his collection.

The publishers would like to thank the following people and organisations listed below for permission to reproduce the photographs in this book. Every care has been taken to trace copyright holders, but any omissions will, if notified, be corrected in any future edition.

All photographs are © English Heritage.NMR with the exception of the following:
By permission of the British Library: Front cover (Roy.14.E.IV. f.244v); p.17 (Add. 42130. f.176v); p.22 (Add. 42130 f.163v); p. 74 (Add. 42130 f.206v).
By permission of Derry Brabbs: pp. 11; 24; 59: Andrew Tyner p.73.

Line illustrations by Peter Brears.

RECIPE INDEX